Ready, Set, Grow!

A Book About Nature

formerly titled *How Things Grow*

By Nancy Buss
Illustrated by Kathy Allert

A GOLDEN BOOK • NEW YORK

Western Publishing Company, Inc., Racine, Wisconsin 53404

MCMXCII

Things are changing around you all the time.
As winter turns to spring, and then to summer, and
then to fall, every living thing in the entire world
is changing. Plants are changing. Animals are
changing.

Look and you can see some of these changes.

A meadow is a good place to look for changes. Here, in the springtime, small white flowers grow close to the ground. When these flowers die, tiny green berries are left behind. In just a few days, the berries change and grow until they are red strawberries, juicy and sweet.

That's when the chipmunk thinks they're good to eat.

You can see other changes if a pond is nearby. You can catch some tadpoles in a jar and watch them as they grow.

At first the tadpoles are like tiny black fish that swim underwater.

But as they grow, they change. Back legs appear, then front legs. And as their legs grow bigger, their tails begin to shrink. The tails grow smaller each day until they completely disappear.

Now the tadpoles are frogs—frogs that hop on the ground, breathe the air, and catch flies for their supper.

A garden, too, is full of changing, growing things.
Here, in the summer, thin white seeds begin
turning into pumpkins. There are many changes
along the way. Plant some pumpkin seeds and see.

Soon after the seeds are planted, the first leaves appear. More and more leaves follow—and flowers, too. Some of the flowers have long stems. Other flowers have short stems with small green bumps. When these flowers die, the bumps grow bigger and rounder, and start to change color.

When the pumpkins are ripe, you can make changes, too.

It is easy to see how a pumpkin grows or how a tadpole becomes a frog. But there are some changes that are hard to see.

Hen's eggs hatch, and out come baby chicks that peep and scurry in the dirt. How does that happen?

If you could look inside the eggshell, you would see a spot on the yellow part of the egg. That spot can become a baby chicken.

As the mother hen warms the egg, the tiny spot grows. The yellow part—or yolk—is food for the growing chick.

Each day the chick grows bigger, and each day it looks more like a bird.

After three weeks, the egg is ready to hatch.

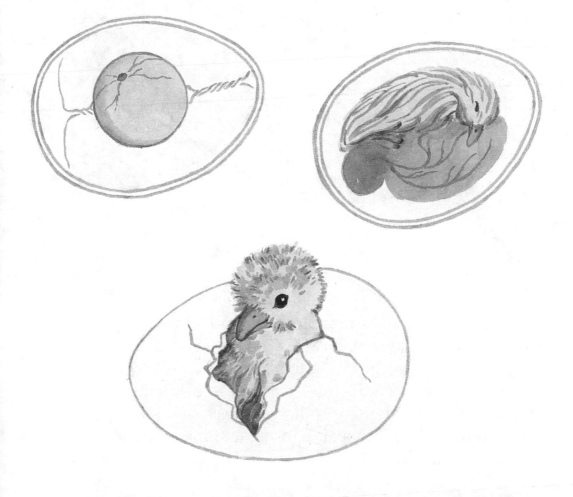

Caterpillars come from eggs, too. But they grow and change in a different way.

The egg hatches on a leaf. Then the caterpillar eats the leaf. It eats another, and another, and another, and the caterpillar grows.

When it's as big as it can be, it spins a cocoon around itself.

Inside the cocoon, it changes some more.

Trees change, too. They don't start out big.
A tiny seed falls from a pine cone onto the forest floor, and becomes a small seedling.

If the sun warms it, and if the rains water it, the little tree will grow. It won't grow quickly. You'll hardly notice the change. But in five years, the small tree will be almost as tall as you are now. In ten years, it will reach far over your head. And in twenty years, it will be a very big tree indeed.

And while that tree is growing, you will also be growing. For you are changing, too.

You were once a tiny baby. You couldn't walk or talk. You couldn't run or play.

Now you are big. You have learned to do lots of things by yourself. And every day you learn more, and every day you do things better.

Because each day, and each week, and each year,
you are becoming more and more the special
person you are meant to be. And that's the most
wonderful change of all!